W9-BEL-661

EVERYTHING I NEED TO KNOW I LEARNED FROM

LED-ZEPPELIN

Everything I Need to Know I Learned From LED-ZEPPELIN

LAUGHING ELEPHANT

THE ENTHUSIAST publishes books, gifts and paper goods. Subjects include, vintage how-to, retro-cooking and home economics, holidays and celebrations, games and puzzles, graphic design, classic children's literature & humor.

Copyright © 2016, The Enthusiast
Second Printing. Printed in China. All rights reserved.
No part of this book may be reproduced in any form without permission in writing from the publisher.

ISBN/EAN: 9781942334132

LAUGHING ELEPHANT
3645 Interlake Avenue North • Seattle • Washington • 98103

LAUGHINGELEPHANT.COM

"Well, I sort of don't trust anybody who doesn't like Led Zeppelin."

–JACK WHITE

"Heavy Metal would not exist without Led Zeppelin,
and if it did, it would suck."

–DAVE GROHL

"Hey, I believe in God, man. I've seen him, I've felt his power. He plays
drums for Led Zeppelin and his name is John Bonham, baby!

–NICK ANDOPOLIS, FREAKS AND GEEKS

"When it comes down to making out, whenever possible, put on Side One of
Led Zeppelin IV."

–DAMONE, FAST TIMES AT RIDGEMONT HIGH

"Led Zeppelin, the greatest rock and roll band of all time"

–JACK BLACK

"I may not believe in myself, but I believe in what I'm doing."
– Jimmy Page

"Don't be hard on yourself. And take as many chances, risks, as you can."
– Robert Plant

Led Zeppelin:
the Experience of Life
and the Pursuit of Dreams

Ramble On! Led Zeppelin tells us, emphatically, now's the time, the time is NOW!

Led Zeppelin encourages us to follow our heart, to find the queen of all our dreams, but also to embrace the inherent dualism in our lives; to live for our dreams *and* a pocketful of gold. In short, we can seek success and be true to ourselves as well. The essential message from Led Zeppelin is to get out there and take chances, recognize and follow our hearts desires, and bravely embrace life.
Mistakes will be made, of course. We will crawl, and wail, and accept that upon us all, a little rain must fall. We will wonder how much there is to know, and whether all that glitters is indeed gold, or merely a mirage. It's all part of the great mysterious magic of life. We are after all, Golden Gods.

However you decide to take this trip, you must remember that yes, there are two paths you can go by, but in the long run, there's still time to change the road you're on.

Recomended Listening for Section One:
Ramble On
The Immigrant Song
Kashmir
And of course.... Stairway to Heaven

Oh! let the sun
beat down upon my face

With stars to fill my
dreams

I am a traveller
of both time and space
to be where I have been

Yes there are two paths
you can go by,
but in the long run...

Hey It's lonely at the bottom
Man, it's dizzy at the top

But when you're standing
in the middle,

Ain't no way you gonna
stop

Many times I've wondered how much there is to know

Your head is humming
and it won't go,
in case you don't know

The Piper's callin' you
to join him

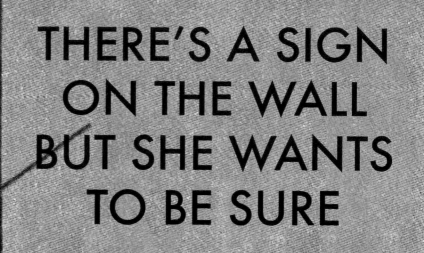

And if you listen very hard

The tune will
come to you at last

When all are one
and one is all

Sit and Wait,

...all will be revealed

Whatever that
your days may bring

There's no use hiding
in the corner

Honey that won't
change a thing

This is the mystery of
the quotient, quotient

Upon us all, upon us all,
a little rain must fall

Many is a word,
that only leaves you
guessing

Guessing 'bout a thing,
you really ought to know

If you're dancing in
the doldrums

One day soon it's got to stop,
it's got to stop

When you're master
of the off-chance,
well, you don't expect a lot

Many dreams come true,
and some have silver linings

I live for my dream,
and a pocketful of gold

So now you better stop and rebuild all your ruins...

...For peace and trust
can win the day
despite of all you're losing

I'M JUST A SIMPLE GUY,
AND I LIVE FROM DAY TO DAY
A RAY OF SUNSHINE MELTS MY FROWN,
BLOWS MY BLUES AWAY

> "*I think that passion and love and pain are all bearable, and they go to make love beautiful.*"

-Robert Plant

> "*I'm just looking for an angel with a broken wing.*"

-Jimmy Page

Led Zeppelin:
Love and Romance

Led Zeppelin Loves passionately! Not only do they sing of romantic love that eternally lives on, even if the sun refused to shine, but of love for family and friends as well. By urging us and those we love to find the light and offer to share the load, Led Zeppelin implores us to love in expansive and collective ways for the good of the planet. Sometimes, the greatest thing you ever can do, now, is trade a smile with someone who is blue now...

Love is also a source of pain, a thousand years can pass from when she was your queen. It bites us, and pushes us to unimaginable limits, but ultimately, love is our reality, and it's power holds great meaning. It is worth the sacrifice, it is worth crawling for.

Led Zeppelin, despite all the legends, are romantics, they believe that the winter of loneliness will end because they know that they love you so, and offer, quite simply, all of their love, as we all should.

Reccomended Listening for Section Two:
Thank You
The Rain Song
Tangerine
all of my love

And so, today,
my world it smiles

Your hand in mine,
we walk the miles

Thanks to you
it will be done

For you to me are
the only one

Hey Lady,
you've got the love I need

Maybe, more than enough

Oh Darlin' Darlin' Darlin'
walk a while with me...

I'm telling you now

the greatest thing you ever
can do, now

Is trade a smile with
someone who's blue, now

It's very easy, just a...

We are eagles of one nest,
the nest is in our soul

IF THE SUN REFUSED TO SHINE
I WOULD STILL BE LOVING YOU
WHEN MOUNTAINS CRUMBLE TO THE SEA
THERE WILL STILL BE YOU & ME

Many have I loved,
and many times been bitten

Many times I've gazed
along the open road

It is the Summer of
my smiles
Flee from me, keepers of
the gloom

Speak to me only with
your eyes,
It is to you I give
this tune

STAIRWAY TO HEAVEN

Spirituality

3

"I have a voracious appetite for all things, worldly and unworldly."
-JIMMY PAGE

"You have to ask these questions: who pays the piper, and what is valuable in this life?"
-ROBERT PLANT

"We are trying to communicate a fulfilled ideal. Does anybody remember laughter?"
-ROBERT PLANT

LED ZEPPELIN:
THE GOLDEN GODS, THIER HAMMERS,
AND ALL THAT IS HOLY

Led Zeppelin are, perhaps even more than they are lovers and dreamers, mystics. They are deeply spiritual, pagan and earthy. They see God, or more appropriately, The Goddess, in all things, and seek to be in harmony with Lady Nature; to dance in the dark of night and sing to the morning light. They sing loud for the sunshine and pray hard for the rain. Led Zeppelin looks forward to an enlightenment and spiritual awakening amongst all of mankind. They tell us to show our love for Lady Nature and she will come back again; that a piper will lead us to reason; a new day will dawn for those who stand long and the forests will echo with laughter. What a nice thought for these troubled times.
There is a universal thread of spirituality in all of Led Zeppelin's music, interwoven with great respect, love, and reverance for the Divine.

RECCOMENDED LISTENING FOR SECTION THREE:

DOWN BY THE SEASIDE
IN THE LIGHT
STAIRWAY TO HEAVEN

Sing loud for the sunshine,
pray hard for the rain

And show your love
for Lady Nature and
she will come back again

These are the seasons
of emotion

And like the wind,
they rise and fall

EVERYBODY NEEDS A LIGHT!

TO THE BRIDGE →

IF YOU FEEL THAT YOU CAN'T GO ON
AND YOUR WHEEL'S SINKING LOW

GOOD TIMES
BAD TIMES
RAMBLE
ON
JUST BELIEVE & YOU
CAN'T GO WRONG
IN THE LIGHT
YOU WILL FIND
THE ROAD

Then, as it was, then again it will be

And though the course may change sometimes...

...Rivers always reach the sea

So anytime
somebody needs you,

don't let them down,
although it grieves you

Some day you'll need
someone like they do

Looking for what you knew

AND AS THE ROAD
WE WIND ON DOWN
OUR SHADOWS TALLER THAN OUR SOULS
THERE WALKS A LADY WE ALL KNOW WHO
SHINES WHITE LIGHT AND WANTS TO SHOW
HOW EVERYTHING STILL TURNS TO GOLD

DOWN BY THE SEASIDE

DOWN BY THE SEASIDE, SEE THE BOATS GO SAILING
CAN THE PEOPLE HEAR, OH, WHAT THE LITTLE FISH ARE SAYING
AH__OOH__OH, OH THE PEOPLE TURNED AWAY, OH, THE PEOPLE TURNED AWAY

DOWN IN THE CITY STREETS, SEE ALL THE FOLK GO RACING, RACING
NO TIME LEFT, NO, NO, TO PASS THE TIME OF DAY IN
AH__OOH__YEAH, YEAH, THE PEOPLE TURNED AWAY, PEOPLE TURNED AWAY
SO FAR AWAY, SO FAR AWAY
SEE HOW THEY RUN, SEE HOW THEY RUN, SEE HOW THEY RUN,

CAN YOU STILL DO THE TWIST
DO YOU FIND THAT YOU REMEMBER THINGS THAT WELL
SOME FOLK TWISTING EVERY DAY
THOUGH SOMETIMES IT'S AWFUL HARD TO TELL, AH, HA

OUT IN THE COUNTRY, HEAR THE PEOPLE SINGING
SINGING 'BOUT THE GROWING, KNOWING WHERE THEY'RE GOING
YEAH, YEAH, THEY KNOW, YEAH, THEY KNOW
AH__OOH__OH, OH THE PEOPLE TURNED AWAY, OH, THE PEOPLE TURNED AWAY

SING LOUD FOR THE SUNSHINE, PRAY HARD FOR THE RAIN
AND SHOW YOUR LOVE FOR LADY NATURE AND SHE WILL COME BACK AGAIN
AH__OOH__OH, OH THE PEOPLE TURNED AWAY, OH, THE PEOPLE TURNED AWAY
DON'T THEY KNOW THAT THEY'RE GOING

FRIENDS

BRIGHT LIGHT, ALMOST BLINDING, BLACK NIGHT STILL THERE SHINING
I CAN'T STOP, KEEP ON CLIMBING, LOOKING FOR WHAT I KNEW
HAD A FRIEND, SHE ONCE TOLD ME, "YOU GOT A LOVE, YOU AIN'T LONELY"
NOW SHE'S GONE AND LEFT ME ONLY, LOOKING FOR WHAT I KNEW

MMM, I'M TELLING YOU, NOW
THE GREATEST THING YOU EVER CAN DO, NOW
IS TRADE A SMILE WITH SOMEONE WHO'S BLUE, NOW
IT'S VERY EASY, JUST-A

MET A MAN ON THE ROADSIDE CRYING,
WITHOUT A FRIEND, THERE'S NO DENYING
YOU'RE INCOMPLETE, THERE'LL BE NO FINDING,
LOOKING FOR WHAT YOU KNEW
SO ANYTIME SOMEBODY NEEDS YOU
DON'T LET THEM DOWN, ALTHOUGH IT GRIEVES YOU
SOMEDAY YOU'LL NEED SOMEONE LIKE THEY DO,
LOOKING FOR WHAT YOU KNEW

I'M TELLING YOU, NOW, THE GREATEST THING YOU EVER CAN DO, NOW
IS TRADE A SMILE WITH SOMEONE WHO'S BLUE, NOW
IT'S VERY EASY, IT'S VERY EASY, IT'S EASY, EASY YEAH

IMMIGRANT SONG

AH___AH___ WE COME FROM THE LAND OF THE ICE AND SNOW
FROM THE MIDNIGHT SUN WHERE THE HOT SPRINGS BLOW

THE HAMMER OF THE GODS WILL DRIVE OUR SHIPS TO NEW LANDS
TO FIGHT THE HORDE AND SING AND CRY, "VALHALLA, I AM COMING"

ON WE SWEEP WITH, WITH THRESHING OAR
OUR ONLY GOAL WILL BE THE WESTERN SHORE

AH___AH___ WE COME FROM THE LAND OF THE ICE AND SNOW
FROM THE MIDNIGHT SUN WHERE THE HOT SPRINGS BLOW

HOW SOFT YOUR FIELDS, SO GREEN
CAN WHISPER TALES OF GORE, OF HOW WE CALMED THE TIDES OF WAR
WE ARE YOUR OVERLORDS

ON WE SWEEP WITH THRESHING OAR,
OUR ONLY GOAL WILL BE THE WESTERN SHORE

SO NOW YOU BETTER STOP AND REBUILD ALL YOUR RUINS
FOR PEACE AND TRUST CAN WIN THE DAY DESPITE OF ALL YOU'RE LOSING

IN THE EVENING

IN THE EVENING,
WHEN THE DAY IS DONE
I'M LOOKING FOR A WOMAN
OH, BUT THE GIRL DON'T COME
SO DON'T LET HER
PLAY YOU FOR NO FOOL
SHE WON'T SHOW NO PITY, BABY
YOU KNOW THAT SHE DON'T MAKE NO RULE

OH, I NEED YOUR LOVE, I NEED YOUR LOVE
OH, I NEED YOUR LOVE, I'VE JUST GOTTA HAVE

SO DON'T YOU LET HER
OH, GET UNDER YOUR SKIN
IT'S ONLY BAD LUCK AND TROUBLE
OH, FROM THE DAY THAT YOU BEGIN
I HEAR YOU CRYING IN THE DARKNESS
DON'T ASK NOBODY'S HELP
OH AIN'T NO POCKETS FULL OF MERCY BABY
'CAUSE YOU CAN ONLY BLAME YOURSELF

OH, I NEED YOUR LOVE, OH, OH, I NEED YOUR LOVE
OOH, YEAH, I NEED YOUR LOVE, I'VE GOTTA HAVE

OOH, IT'S SIMPLE,
ALL THE PAIN THAT YOU'LL GO THROUGH
YOU CAN'T TURN AWAY FROM FORTUNE, FORTUNE, FORTUNE,
'CAUSE THAT'S ALL THAT'S LEFT TO YOU
HEY, IT'S LONELY AT THE BOTTOM, MAN, IT'S DIZZY AT THE TOP
BUT WHEN YOU'RE STANDING IN THE MIDDLE
AIN'T NO WAY YOU GONNA STOP

OH, I NEED YOUR LOVE, OH, I NEED YOUR LOVE, OH, I NEED YOUR LOVE,
I'VE GOTTA HAVE

WHATEVER
THAT YOUR DAYS MAY BRING
THERE'S NO USE HIDING IN THE CORNER,
HONEY THAT WON'T CHANGE A THING
IF YOU'RE DANCING IN THE DOLDRUMS
ONE DAY SOON IT'S GOT TO STOP, IT'S GOT TO STOP
WHEN YOU'RE MASTER OF THE OFF-CHANCE
WELL YOU DON'T EXPECT A LOT

IN THE LIGHT

AND IF YOU FEEL THAT YOU CAN'T GO ON, AND YOUR WHEEL'S SINKING LOW
JUST BELIEVE, AND YOU CAN'T GO WRONG
IN THE LIGHT YOU WILL FIND THE ROAD, YOU WILL FIND THE ROAD

DID YOU EVER BELIEVE THAT I COULD LEAVE YOU, STANDING OUT IN THE COLD
HEY YEAH, BABY, I KNOW HOW IT FEELS 'CAUSE I HAVE SLIPPED THROUGH
TO THE VERY DEPTHS OF MY SOUL, YEAH
OH, BABY, I JUST WANNA SHOW YOU WHAT A CLEAR VIEW
THERE IS FROM EVERY BEND IN THE ROAD NOW
NOW LISTEN TO ME, OH
WHOA, AS (IT WAS FOR ME) IT WILL BE FOR YOU TOO, HONEY
AS YOU WOULD FOR ME, I WILL SHARE YOUR LOAD
LET ME SHARE YOUR LOAD, OOH, LET ME SHARE, SHARE YOUR LOAD

AND IF YOU FEEL THAT YOU CAN'T GO ON
IN THE LIGHT YOU WILL FIND THE ROAD
HEY, UH, OH, THE WINDS OF CHANGE MAY BLOW AROUND YOU
BUT THAT WILL ALWAYS BE SO
OH WHOA, WHOA, WHEN LOVE IS PAIN, IT CAN DEVOUR YOU
BUT YOU ARE NEVER ALONE
I WILL SHARE YOUR LOAD I WILL SHARE YOUR LOAD, BABY, LET ME, OH, LET ME
IN THE LIGHT EVERYBODY NEEDS A LIGHT, OOH YEAH
OOH, BABY, EVERYBODY, EVERYBODY, EVERYBODY, SURE 'NUFF THEY DO

KASHMIR

OH! LET THE SUN BEAT DOWN UPON MY FACE
WITH STARS TO FILL MY DREAMS
I AM A TRAVELER OF BOTH TIME AND SPACE
TO BE WHERE I HAVE BEEN
TO SIT WITH ELDERS OF A GENTLE RACE
THIS WORLD HAS SELDOM SEEN
WHO TALK OF DAYS FOR WHICH THEY SIT IN WAIT
WHEN ALL WILL BE REVEALED

WITH TALK AND SONG FROM TONGUES OF LILTING GRACE
THE SOUNDS CARESS MY EAR
THOUGH NOT A WORD I HEARD COULD I RELATE
THE STORY WAS QUITE CLEAR
OOOH, OH, BABY, I'VE BEEN FLYIN' LORD YEAH
MAMA, THERE AIN'T NO DENYIN'
OH, YES, I'VE BEEN FLYIN'
MAMA, MAMA, AIN'T NO DENYIN', NO DENYIN', NO

OH, ALL I SEE TURNS TO BROWN, AS THE SUN BURNS THE GROUND
AND MY EYES FILL WITH SAND, AS I SCAN THIS WASTED LAND
TRYING TO FIND, TRYING TO FIND WHERE I'VE BEEN

OH, PILOT OF THE STORM WHO LEAVES NO TRACE
LIKE THOUGHTS INSIDE A DREAM
WHO HID THE PATH THAT LED ME TO THAT PLACE
WITH YELLOW DESERT SCREEN

MY SHANGRI-LA BENEATH THE SUMMER MOON, I WILL RETURN AGAIN
SURE AS THE DUST THAT BLOWS HIGH IN JUNE
WHEN MOVING THROUGH KASHMIR

OH, FATHER OF THE FOUR WINDS, FILL MY SAILS
TO CROSS THE SEA OF YEARS
WITH NO PROVISION BUT AN OPEN FACE TO FLAUNT THE STRAITS OF FEAR
WHOA___ OH___
WELL, WHEN I'M ON, WHEN I'M ON MY WAY
WHEN I SEE, WHEN I SEE THE WAY YOU STAY, YEAH
OOH, YEAH, OOH, YEAH, WHEN I'M DOWN, OH
OOH, YEAH, OOH, YEAH, WHEN I'M DOWN, SO DOWN
OOH, MY BABY, OOH, MY BABY, LET ME TAKE YOU THERE
OOH, COME ON, COME ON, OH, LET ME TAKE YOU THERE
OOH, YEAH, OOH, YEAH

OUT ON THE TILES

AS I WALK DOWN THE HIGHWAY, ALL I DO IS SING A SONG
AND A TRAIN THAT'S PASSING MY WAY HELPS THE RHYTHM MOVE ALONG
THERE IS NO DOUBT ABOUT, THE WORDS ARE CLEAR
THE VOICE IS STRONG, IT'S OH, SO STRONG

I'M JUST A SIMPLE GUY, AND I LIVE FROM DAY TO DAY
A RAY OF SUNSHINE MELTS MY FROWN, BLOWS MY BLUES AWAY
THERE'S NOTHING MORE THAT I CAN SAY
BUT ON A DAY LIKE TODAY, I PASS THE TIME AWAY
AND WALK A QUIET MILE WITH YOU

ALL I NEED FROM YOU, IS ALL YOUR LOVE
ALL YOU GOT TO GIVE TO ME IS ALL YOUR LOVE
ALL I NEED FROM YOU, IS ALL YOUR LOVE
ALL YOU GOT TO GIVE TO ME, IS ALL YOUR LOVE
OOH, YEAH, OOH, YEAH, OOH, YEAH, OOH, YEAH

I'M SO GLAD I'M LIVING, (STOP), GONNA TELL THE WORLD I AM
I GOT ME A FINE WOMAN, AND SHE SAYS THAT I'M HER MAN
ONE THING THAT I KNOW FOR SURE
GONNA GIVE HER ALL THE LOVING
LIKE NOBODY, NOBODY, NOBODY, NOBODY CAN

STAND IN THE NOON-DAY SUN TRYING TO FLAG A RIDE
PEOPLE GO AND PEOPLE COME, SEE MY RIDER RIGHT BY MY SIDE
IT'S A TOTAL DISGRACE, THEY SET THE PACE
IT MUST BE A RACE
THE BEST THING I CAN DO IS RUN

ALL I NEED FROM YOU IS ALL YOUR LOVE
ALL YOU GOTTA GIVE TO ME IS ALL YOUR LOVE
ALL I NEED FROM YOU IS ALL YOUR LOVE
ALL YOU GOTTA GIVE TO ME IS ALL YOUR LOVE

AW, YEAH, AW, YEAH, AW, YEAH
ALL THAT THE RHYTHM SAID WAS KEEP ON
ALL THAT RHYTHM SAID WAS KEEP ON

OVER THE HILLS AND FAR AWAY

HEY, LADY, YOU GOT THE LOVE I NEED
MAYBE, MORE THAN ENOUGH
OH, DARLIN', DARLIN', DARLIN', WALK A WHILE WITH ME
OH___YOU GOT SO MUCH, SO MUCH, SO MUCH

MANY HAVE I LOVED, AND MANY TIMES BEEN BITTEN
AND MANY TIMES I'VE GAZED ALONG THE OPEN ROAD
MANY TIMES I'VE LIED AND MANY TIMES I'VE LISTENED
MANY TIMES I'VE WONDERED HOW MUCH THERE IS TO KNOW
MANY DREAMS COME TRUE, AND SOME HAVE SILVER LININGS
I LIVE FOR MY DREAM AND A POCKETFUL OF GOLD

MELLOW IS THE MAN WHO KNOWS WHAT HE'S BEEN MISSING
MANY, MANY MEN CAN'T SEE THE OPEN ROAD
MANY IS A WORD THAT ONLY LEAVES YOU GUESSING
GUESSING 'BOUT A THING YOU REALLY OUGHT TO KNOW
OH, OH, OH, OH,
REALLY OUGHT TO KNOW, OH, OH,
I REALLY OUGHT TO KNOW
OH YOU KNOW I SHOULD, YOU KNOW I SHOULD, YOU KNOW I SHOULD DARLIN'

THE RAIN SONG

IT IS THE SPRINGTIME OF MY LOVING
THE SECOND SEASON I AM TO KNOW
YOU ARE THE SUNLIGHT IN MY GROWING
SO LITTLE WARMTH I FELT BEFORE
IT ISN'T HARD TO FEEL ME GLOWING
I WATCHED THE FIRE THAT GREW SO LOW, OH____

IT IS THE SUMMER OF MY SMILES
FLEE FROM ME, KEEPERS OF THE GLOOM
SPEAK TO ME ONLY WITH YOUR EYES
IT IS TO YOU I GIVE THIS TUNE
AIN'T SO HARD TO RECOGNIZE, OH___
THESE THINGS ARE CLEAR TO ALL FROM TIME TO TIME OH____

UH, OH, UH
UH TALK, TALK, TALK, TALK
I FELT THE COLDNESS OF MY WINTER
I NEVER THOUGHT IT WOULD EVER GO
I CURSED THE GLOOM THAT SET UPON US, 'PON US, 'PON US
BUT I KNOW THAT I LOVE YOU SO
OH-WHOA, BUT I KNOW THAT I LOVE YOU SO

THESE ARE THE SEASONS OF EMOTION
AND LIKE THE WIND, THEY RISE AND FALL
THIS IS THE WONDER OF DEVOTION
I SEE THE TORCH WE ALL MUST HOLD
THIS IS THE MYSTERY OF THE QUOTIENT, QUOTIENT
UPON US ALL, UPON US ALL, A LITTLE RAIN MUST FALL
JUST A LITTLE RAIN, OH

STAIRWAY To HEAVEN

THERE'S A LADY WHO'S SURE ALL THAT GLITTERS IS GOLD
AND SHE'S BUYING A STAIRWAY To HEAVEN
WHEN SHE GETS THERE, SHE KNOWS IF THE STORES ARE ALL CLOSED
WITH A WORD SHE CAN GET WHAT SHE CAME FOR
OOH___ AND SHE'S BUYING A STAIRWAY To HEAVEN

THERE'S A SIGN ON THE WALL, BUT SHE WANTS To BE SURE,
'CAUSE YOU KNOW SOMETIMES WORDS HAVE TWO MEANINGS
IN A TREE BY THE BROOK, THERE'S A SONGBIRD WHO SINGS
SOMETIMES ALL OF OUR THOUGHTS ARE MISGIVEN

OOH___ IT MAKES ME WONDER, OOH___ MAKES ME WONDER

THERE'S A FEELING I GET WHEN I LOOK To THE WEST
AND MY SPIRIT IS CRYING FOR LEAVING
IN MY THOUGHTS I HAVE SEEN RINGS OF SMOKE THROUGH THE TREES
AND THE VOICES OF THOSE WHO STAND LOOKING

OOH___ IT MAKES ME WONDER, OOH____ IT REALLY MAKES ME WONDER

AND IT'S WHISPERED THAT SOON, IF WE ALL CALL THE TUNE
THEN THE PIPER WILL LEAD US To REASON
AND A NEW DAY WILL DAWN FOR THOSE WHO STAND LONG

AND THE FORESTS WILL ECHO WITH LAUGHTER

IF THERE'S A BUSTLE IN YOUR HEDGEROW, DON'T BE ALARMED, NOW
IT'S JUST A SPRING CLEAN FOR THE MAY QUEEN
YES, THERE ARE TWO PATHS YOU CAN GO BY, BUT IN THE LONG RUN
THERE'S STILL TIME TO CHANGE THE ROAD YOU'RE ON

AND IT MAKES ME WONDER OH___

YOUR HEAD IS HUMMING AND IT WON'T GO, IN CASE YOU DON'T KNOW
THE PIPER'S CALLING YOU TO JOIN HIM
DEAR LADY, CAN YOU HEAR THE WIND BLOW, AND DID YOU KNOW
YOUR STAIRWAY LIES ON THE WHISPERING WIND

AND AS WE WIND ON DOWN THE ROAD
OUR SHADOWS TALLER THAN OUR SOUL
THERE WALKS A LADY WE ALL KNOW
WHO SHINES WHITE LIGHT AND WANTS TO SHOW
HOW EVERYTHING STILL TURNS TO GOLD
AND IF YOU LISTEN VERY HARD
THE TUNE WILL COME TO YOU AT LAST
WHEN ALL ARE ONE AND ONE IS ALL, YEAH
TO BE A ROCK AND NOT TO ROLL
AND SHE'S BUYING A STAIRWAY TO HEAVEN

TEN YEARS GONE

THEN, AS IT WAS, THEN AGAIN IT WILL BE
AND THOUGH THE COURSE MAY CHANGE SOMETIMES,
RIVERS ALWAYS REACH THE SEA

FLYING SKIES OF FORTUNE, EACH OUR SEPARATE WAYS,
ON THE WINGS OF MAYBE, DOWNY BIRDS OF PREY
KIND OF MAKES ME FEEL SOMETIMES, WE DIDN'T HAVE TO GROW,
BUT AS THE EAGLE LEAVES THE NEST, HE'S GOT SO FAR TO GO

CHANGES FILL MY TIME
BABY, THAT'S ALL RIGHT WITH ME
IN THE MIDST, I THINK OF YOU AND HOW IT USED TO BE

DID YOU EVER REALLY NEED SOMEBODY AND REALLY NEED THEM BAD
DID YOU EVER REALLY WANT SOMEBODY, THE BEST LOVE YOU EVER HAD
DO YOU EVER REMEMBER ME, BABY, DID IT FEEL SO GOOD
'CAUSE IT WAS JUST THE FIRST TIME, AND YOU KNEW YOU WOULD

DEWY EYES NOW SPARKLE, SENSES GROWING KEEN
TASTE THE LOVE ALONG THE WAY, SEE YOUR FEATHERS PREEN
KIND OF MAKES ME FEEL SOMETIMES, DIDN'T HAVE TO GO
WE ARE EAGLES OF ONE NEST, THE NEST IS IN OUR SOUL

FIXING IN MY DREAMS, WITH GREAT SURPRISE TO ME
NEVER THOUGHT I'D SEE YOUR FACE THE WAY IT USED TO BE
OH, DARLING, OH DARLING, OH__ OH DARLING, HEY YEAH, OH DARLING,
I'M NEVER GONNA LEAVE YOU, I'M NEVER GONNA LEAVE YOU
TEN YEARS GONE, HOLDIN' ON, TEN YEARS GONE

THANK YOU

IF THE SUN REFUSED TO SHINE, I WOULD STILL BE LOVING YOU
WHEN MOUNTAINS CRUMBLE TO THE SEA
THERE WILL STILL BE YOU AND ME
KIND WOMAN, I GIVE YOU MY ALL, KIND WOMAN, NOTHING MORE

LITTLE DROPS OF RAIN WHISPER OF THE PAIN
TEARS OF LOVES LOST IN THE DAYS GONE BY
MY LOVE IS STRONG, WITH YOU THERE IS NO WRONG
TOGETHER WE SHALL GO UNTIL WE DIE, OH, MY, MY
AN INSPIRATION'S WHAT YOU ARE TO ME, INSPIRATION, LOOK, SEE

AND SO TODAY MY WORLD, IT SMILES
YOUR HAND IN MINE, WE WALK THE MILES
THANKS TO YOU, IT WILL BE DONE,
FOR YOU TO ME ARE THE ONLY ONE, ALL RIGHT, YEAH
HAPPINESS, NO MORE BE SAD, HAPPINESS, I'M GLAD

IF THE SUN REFUSED TO SHINE, I WOULD STILL BE LOVING YOU
MOUNTAINS CRUMBLE TO THE SEA, THERE WILL STILL BE YOU AND ME

TEN YEARS GONE
Music and Lyrics by JIMMY PAGE and ROBERT PLANT
© 1975 (Renewed) FLAMES OF ALBION MUSIC, INC. All Rights Administered by WB MUSIC CORP.
Exclusive Print Rights for the World Excluding Europe Administered by ALFRED MUSIC All Rights Reserved

STAIRWAY TO HEAVEN
Music and Lyrics by JIMMY PAGE and ROBERT PLANT
© 1972 (Renewed) FLAMES OF ALBION MUSIC, INC. All Rights Administered by WB MUSIC CORP.
Exclusive Print Rights for the World Excluding Europe Administered by ALFRED MUSIC All Rights Reserved

IMMIGRANT SONG
Music and Lyrics by JIMMY PAGE and ROBERT PLANT
© 1970 (Renewed) FLAMES OF ALBION MUSIC, INC. All Rights Administered by WB MUSIC CORP.
Exclusive Print Rights for the World Excluding Europe Administered by ALFRED MUSIC All Rights Reserved

OVER THE HILLS AND FAR AWAY
Music and Lyrics by JIMMY PAGE and ROBERT PLANT
© 1973 (Renewed) FLAMES OF ALBION MUSIC, INC. All Rights Administered by WB MUSIC CORP.
Exclusive Print Rights for the World Excluding Europe Administered by ALFRED MUSIC All Rights Reserved

IN THE LIGHT
Music and Lyrics by JIMMY PAGE, ROBERT PLANT and JOHN PAUL JONES
© 1975 (Renewed) FLAMES OF ALBION MUSIC, INC. All Rights Administered by WB MUSIC CORP.
Exclusive Print Rights for the World Excluding Europe Administered by ALFRED MUSIC All Rights Reserved

FRIENDS
Words and Music by JIMMY PAGE and ROBERT PLANT
© 1970 (Renewed) FLAMES OF ALBION MUSIC, INC. All Rights Administered by WB MUSIC CORP.
Exclusive Print Rights for the World Excluding Europe Administered by ALFRED MUSIC All Rights Reserved

DOWN BY THE SEASIDE
Words and Music by JIMMY PAGE, ROBERT PLANT
© 1975 (Renewed) FLAMES OF ALBION MUSIC, INC. All Rights Administered by WB MUSIC CORP.
Exclusive Print Rights for the World Excluding Europe Administered by ALFRED MUSIC All Rights Reserved

KASHMIR
Words and Music by JIMMY PAGE, ROBERT PLANT and JOHN BONHAM
© 1975 (Renewed) FLAMES OF ALBION MUSIC, INC. All Rights Administered by WB MUSIC CORP.
Exclusive Print Rights for the World Excluding Europe Administered by ALFRED MUSIC All Rights Reserved

IN THE EVENING
Words and Music by JOHN PAUL JONES, JIMMY PAGE and ROBERT PLANT
© 1979 FLAMES OF ALBION MUSIC, INC. All Rights Administered by WB MUSIC CORP.
Exclusive Print Rights for the World Excluding Europe Administered by ALFRED MUSIC All Rights Reserved

THANK YOU
Music and Lyrics by JIMMY PAGE and ROBERT PLANT
© 1969 (Renewed) FLAMES OF ALBION MUSIC, INC. All Rights Administered by WB MUSIC CORP.
Exclusive Print Rights for the World Excluding Europe Administered by ALFRED MUSIC All Rights Reserved

OUT ON THE TILES
Words and Music by JIMMY PAGE, ROBERT PLANT and JOHN BONHAM
© 1970 (Renewed) FLAMES OF ALBION MUSIC, INC. All Rights Administered by WB MUSIC CORP.
Exclusive Print Rights for the World Excluding Europe Administered by ALFRED MUSIC All Rights Reserved

RAIN SONG, THE
Words and Music by JIMMY PAGE and ROBERT PLANT
© 1973 (Renewed) FLAMES OF ALBION MUSIC, INC. All Rights Administered by WB MUSIC CORP.
Exclusive Print Rights for the World Excluding Europe Administered by ALFRED MUSIC All Rights Reserved

PHOTOGRAPHS
Courtesy of Heinrich Klaffs

SPECIAL THANKS TO ARTIST
MAX HARPER
FOR THE AMAZING MELTING SKULLS